Dancing

Susan Canizares
Betsey Chessen

Scholastic Inc.

New York • Toronto • London • Auckland • Sydney

Acknowledgments

Literacy Specialist: Linda Cornwell

Social Studies Consultant: Barbara Schubert, Ph.D.

Design: Silver Editions

Photo Research: Silver Editions

Endnotes: Jacqueline Smith

Endnote Illustrations: Anthony Carnabucia

———————————————

Photographs: **Cover:** Cammi Asa/Gamma Liaison; p. 1: (tl) Marty Loken/Tony Stone Images; (tr) N. Richmond; (bl) Giboux/Gamma Liaison; (br) Donovan Reese/Tony Stone Images; p. 2: Cindy Charles/Photo Edit; p. 3: Lawrence Migdale/Tony Stone Images; p. 4: Novosti/Gamma Liaison; p. 5: David Young-Wolff/Photo Edit; p. 6: Marcus Brooke/Tony Stone Images; pp. 7, 11: Martha Cooper/The Viesti Collection.; p. 8: Nicholas DeVore/Tony Stone Images; p. 9: Carl Rosenstein/The Viesti Collection; p. 10: Bruno De Hogues/Tony Stone Images; p. 12: Cammi Asa/Gamma Liaison.

Library of Congress Cataloging-in-Publication Data
Canizares, Susan, 1960-
Dancing/Susan Canizares, Betsey Chessen.
p.cm.--(Social studies emergent readers)
Summary: Simple text and photographs introduce some
of the different types of dancing done by people around the world.
ISBN 0-439-04569-X (pbk.: alk. paper)
1. Folk dancing--Equipment and supplies--Juvenile literature.
[1. Folk dancing. 2. Dance.] I. Chessen, Betsey, 1970-. II. Title. III.Series.
GV1743.C35 1999

793.3'1--dc21

98-53541
CIP AC

5   6   7   8   9   10   08   4 5 6/0

Let's go dancing.

Dancing.

Dancing with baskets.

Dancing.

Dancing with fans.

Dancing.

Dancing with feathers.

Dancing.

Dancing with scarves.

Dancing.

Dancing with hoops.

Let's go dancing together.

Dancing

People dance for different reasons in different cultures. Sometimes it is to worship a god or try to influence events, like bringing rain. Sometimes people dance to celebrate—at a wedding, for example. Sometimes dances are for socializing and allowing people to meet. Sometimes dance is an art to watch and enjoy.

Dancing A classical ballerina seems to fly effortlessly through the air, accompanied by beautiful classical music. But ballet is not effortless at all. It requires hard work and years of training. The dances are based on a system of specific movements and positions, each with its own name.

Dancing with baskets Team dances in a circle are the most common form of African dance, and men usually dance separately from women. Originally, the purpose of many of the dances was to magically influence events—to ensure a good harvest or a successful marriage, or to heal a sick person.

Dancing The men leaping high in the air are the Turkmen of Eastern Europe. The Turkmen used to be nomads who lived in tentlike shelters called yurts. They were sheepherders and warriors. Some Turkmen still wear these traditional high sheepskin hats. And they certainly can still dance the old dances!

Dancing with fans These children are performing a traditional Mexican dance for the Cinco de Mayo (May 5) festival, which celebrates an important battle in Mexican history. Accompanied by the guitars, violins, and trumpets of mariachi bands, Mexican dances are usually fast and happy. Most of them are "couples" dances based on the dances of Mexico's Spanish colonizers, with the men in one line and the women facing them in another.

Dancing These people are performing traditional Scottish Highlands dances. Long ago, Scottish warriors did these dances before a battle for good luck and to get into the fighting spirit. The most famous dance was the Sword Dance, during which the warriors jumped in and out of crossed swords on the ground. They were not allowed to touch the swords because this would bring bad luck.

Dancing with feathers These Native Americans are dancing at a powwow, a social gathering in which different tribes get together to tell stories, dance, and sing. They wear feathers on their clothes as important symbols of power and prestige. The feathers are often worn by warriors who have performed some heroic act.

Dancing Traditional Indian dance has an elaborate system of rules and movements and requires extensive training and discipline. The dancer must have control of every part of her body, including her eyes and every muscle in her face! There are 36 facial expressions to show different emotions.

Dancing with scarves In China traditional dance and drama, music, song, acrobatics, and folklore are all part of opera. Chinese opera is performed outdoors and lasts four hours. An orchestra of traditional Chinese instruments accompanies the performers, and the audience often sings along, shouts, and comments on what is happening. The actors must dance, sing, and perform acrobatic feats. The actors wear embroidered robes with long "water" sleeves or scarves, which they swirl around.

Dancing For special rituals in Burundi, 24 tall drums are placed in a circle around the big central drum. The musicians move in a circle around the drums and take turns beating the central drum. They also take turns stomping their feet and jumping high into the air.

Dancing with hoops The Hoop Dance is one of the oldest powwow dances. It is performed mostly by Pueblo Indian boys in the Southwest. It is a very acrobatic dance—the boys spin and twirl the hoops, weaving them in and out to create patterns in the air. The dance was once used for healing and to bring visions of the future.

Let's go dancing together These Thai children are learning the traditional dances of their country in this school. Classical dance-drama in Thailand goes back three centuries and is actually a combination of theater and dance. For some of the dances, all the performers wear elaborate masks. For others, women wear crowns and headdresses and attach gold nails to their fingers.